STEEL IS THE NEW GOLD

AF518106

STEEL IS THE NEW GOLD

PANKAJ GOEL

Available on amazonkindle

Worldwide Published by

Pendown Press

PREMIUM BUSINESS PUBLISHER

PENDOWN PRESS LLP

An ISO 9001 & ISO 14001 Certified Co.,

Regd. Office: 3767A, Kanhaiya Nagar,
Tri Nagar, Delhi-110035
Ph.: 8130886000, 9650072927
E-mail: info@pendownpress.com
Branch Office: 1A/2A, 20, Hari Sadan, Ansari Road,
Daryaganj, New Delhi-110002
Ph.: 011-45794768
Website: PendownPress.com

Edition: 2025
Price: ₹ 399
ISBN: 978-93-7217-973-6

All Rights Reserved

All the ideas and thoughts in this book are given by the author and he is responsible for the treatise, facts and dialogues used in this book. Author is also responsible for the used pictures and the permission to use them in this book. Copyright of this book is reserved with the author. The publisher does not have any responsibility for the above-mentioned matters. No part of this publication may be reproduced, distributed, or transmitted in any form or by any means, including photocopying, recording, or other electronic or mechanical methods, without the prior written permission of the publisher and author.

Layout and Cover Designed by Pendown Graphics Team
Printed and Bound in India by Thomson Press India Ltd.

Table of Contents

Acknowledgements i

Preface iii

Foreword v

About the Author vii

Part I - Steel: The Present & The Future

Chapter 1: Steel in Everything: From Pin to Plane 1

Chapter 2: The Making of Steel 7

Chapter 3: India vs China: The Usage Gap 13

Chapter 4: Steel Across Industries 19

Chapter 5: Sustainability: Steel vs Plastic 27

Chapter 6: Global Edge & Indian Potential 33

Part II - The Vision: Steel as the New Gold

Chapter 7: Why Steel Will Be the Next Gold 39

Chapter 8: Your Playbook for Scaling in the Steel Industry 45

Chapter 9: The Future We Must Build 53

Acknowledgements

No journey is ever walked alone, and this book is no exception. While my words fill these pages, the spirit and strength behind them come from the people who have stood with me through every step.

First and foremost, I owe everything to my entire **family.** I am grateful to my **parents,** whose values shaped me; to my in-laws for their belief and encouragement, and to my **sister,** whose support was the quiet strength behind my journey. My **father's** guidance, values, and unwavering belief gave me the courage to take risks fearlessly and my **father-in-law's** guidance paved my way into the capital markets, where conviction and boldness are everything.

I am especially grateful to **my dear friend Himanshu Goel,** who stood firmly by my side during the uncertain early days of building from scratch.

To **my wife, Ayushi,** my constant partner in life and in vision, you are the foundation on which all my endeavors rest.

I am deeply grateful to my mentors, **Rahul Jain and Sanjeev Jain,** for their wisdom and for pushing me to grow as an entrepreneur and as a leader.

Two industry stalwarts, **Anil Agarwal of Vedanta** and **Arun Gupta of Bansal Wires,** have been sources of immense inspiration. Their journeys, insights, and generosity in sharing their knowledge have shaped my perspective on steel and its transformative role in India's future.

A special thanks to my colleague, **Snover Sanduja,** whose contribution in refining the structure, flow, and message of this book has been invaluable.

Finally, **to every manufacturer, entrepreneur, business owner, and dreamer** I have worked with, you are my teachers. Your struggles, triumphs, and stories of perseverance are what drive me to keep learning and sharing.

This book is dedicated to all of you: the believers, the builders, and the future-makers of India.

Preface

India stands today at the cusp of an economic transformation. Our ambitions, to become a $5 trillion economy, to build world-class infrastructure, to lead in defense and manufacturing, to provide homes and opportunities for millions, will all be tested in the years ahead.

When I look at the industries that will power this growth, one stands above all others: steel.

Steel is in everything we see and touch, from the smallest pin to the tallest skyscraper.

- It builds our homes
- Strengthens our infrastructure
- Powers our factories,
- And defends our borders.

And yet, for far too long, it has remained in the background, quietly indispensable, but rarely celebrated.

This book is my attempt to change that narrative. It is not a technical manual, but a vision.

A vision for how India's entrepreneurs, policymakers, and investors can see steel not as a commodity, but as a strategic opportunity: a new gold for the 21st century.

The chapters ahead combine three strands of my journey:

- My personal experiences working with hundreds of MSMEs as they scaled their businesses.
- My professional understanding of how cash flows, valuations, and financial discipline can unlock growth.
- My conviction that steel will be the backbone of India's next big leap.

My hope is that this book does two things for you: **open your eyes** to the potential of steel and **equip your mind** with ideas on how to participate in this opportunity, whether as an entrepreneur, investor, or policymaker.

If this book inspires even a few readers to think long-term, to invest in industries of necessity, and to build with courage and conviction, I will consider its purpose fulfilled.

~ **Pankaj Goel**

Foreword

In every nation's journey, there comes a time when one industry emerges as the cornerstone of growth.

For India today, that industry is steel.

From infrastructure to defense, from automobiles to renewable energy, steel is not just a material; **it is the backbone of progress.**

Having spent decades in the steel sector, I have seen firsthand how this industry shapes economies, creates jobs, and builds national strength.

Steel is not glamorous like technology or finance, but it is indispensable.

It is in the roads we drive on, the homes we live in, the bridges that connect us, and the industries that power our future. In short, steel is the silent force behind every modern economy.

This is why *Steel is the New Gold* is such a timely and important contribution. Pankaj Goel brings to this subject not just his financial acumen, but also his deep understanding of what drives sustainable business growth.

His perspective is unique: he is not merely looking at steel as an industry insider, but as a visionary who sees the bigger picture, how finance, entrepreneurship, and industry intersect to create long-term value.

I have had the privilege of knowing Pankaj both professionally and personally. person. What stands out about him is not only his expertise in business valuation and cash flow management, but also his dedication to the entrepreneurs he serves. He has the ability to simplify complex financial ideas, guiding MSMEs with clarity and patience. More importantly, his humility, warmth, and genuine desire to see others succeed make him a rare leader in today's fast-paced business world.

This book is more than a reflection on steel—it is a roadmap for how India can harness its steel potential to become a global economic powerhouse.

Pankaj weaves together data, industry insights, and actionable strategies, making this book valuable for entrepreneurs, investors, and policymakers alike.

As you turn these pages, I encourage you to read with both curiosity and conviction. Curiosity to understand the immense opportunities the steel industry holds. Conviction, to believe, as Pankaj does, that India's next leap will be forged in steel.

Steel may not shine like gold, but it builds the foundations of nations. And in the hands of visionary entrepreneurs and leaders, it will shape India's future for decades to come.

~ **Arun Gupta,**

Chairman and Whole-Time Director,

Bansal Wire Industries Ltd

About the Author

Pankaj Goel's journey is one of resilience, vision, and a deep commitment to empowering businesses across India.

Born into a middle-class family, Pankaj grew up with values of integrity, perseverance, and humility, principles instilled by his father that shaped his outlook on life and work. He learned early that while resources may be limited, discipline, patience, and the courage to dream bigger could turn challenges into strengths. These formative lessons became the foundation of his entrepreneurial journey.

Pankaj went on to qualify as a Chartered Accountant, Company Secretary, and Law graduate (LLB); a rare academic combination that gave him a holistic perspective on finance, governance, and regulation.

This strong foundation enabled him to see businesses not merely as numbers on a balance sheet, but as living entities that need clarity, structure, and discipline to thrive.

Over the next 15+ years, Pankaj built a distinguished career across the BFSI sector, investment banking, equity markets, and IPOs. He managed fundraising transactions worth over ₹10,000 crore, spanning private equity, venture capital, institutional investments, and credit. For him, these weren't just financial numbers; they were lifelines for entrepreneurs, fueling growth, enabling expansion, and in many cases, saving businesses from collapse. His most important realization during this period was simple yet powerful: **capital is abundant, but structured access to it is rare.**

This conviction inspired him to establish CapitalSetu, a platform designed to bridge India's capital gap. What began as an invoice discounting and working capital solution quickly grew into something more. Entrepreneurs who approached CapitalSetu seeking liquidity often left with business insights, cash flow discipline frameworks, and growth strategies that transformed their companies. For Pankaj, finance has never been just about money; it has always been about empowering entrepreneurs, scaling businesses, and building industries of necessity.

His vision has been to create a bridge between capital and opportunity, between entrepreneurs and investors, and between India's present and its future.

It was through CapitalSetu's work that Pankaj's conviction about the steel industry deepened. With a substantial portion of his clientele and investment portfolio coming from the sector, he engaged closely with steel businesses and gained firsthand insights into their operations.

He realized that steel is not just a commodity but a force, a material that embodies both traditional strength and modern innovation. Strong enough to build skyscrapers yet adaptable enough for electric vehicles, steel has long been the backbone of industry and is now at the forefront of sustainable, green growth.

For Pankaj, steel symbolizes the very qualities that define great businesses and entrepreneurs: strength, flexibility, affordability, and sustainability. This belief became the foundation of his conviction that steel will be the "new gold" in India's growth story, fueling infrastructure, industry, and innovation for decades to come.

Over the years, Pankaj has been recognized for his leadership and contributions:

- Rising Star Entrepreneur Award
- Recognition by Amity Innovation Incubator
- Nomination by the Hong Kong Trade Development Council for Fintech Innovation
- Selected twice by IIM Ahmedabad's Financial Inclusion Cohort, supported by the Bill & Melinda Gates Foundation

Today, Pankaj continues to guide entrepreneurs with deep expertise in cash flow management, business valuation, and scaling strategies. Through CapitalSetu and his thought leadership in industry forums, he remains driven by one mission: to empower entrepreneurs and position steel as the foundation of India's next big leap.

CHAPTER 1

Steel in Everything: From Pin to Plane

When we say steel is everywhere, it is not a metaphor; it is a literal truth. But beyond the pin and the plane, what truly excites me is the depth of steel's integration into our economy, our society, and our future. It is not just a material that fills gaps; it is the very skeleton that supports modern life.

In this chapter, I want to step beyond the symbolism and explore the real-world presence of steel: the industries it powers, the invisible ways it protects us, and the new-age innovations where steel is proving to be irreplaceable.

Steel in the Built Environment

Let us start with the most visible use of steel: our buildings and cities.

Every skyline that inspires us, from New York to Dubai, from Shanghai to Mumbai, is essentially a portrait painted in steel. Reinforced concrete may get the attention, but the structural heart of modern cities is steel.

- **Skyscrapers:** Without steel, high-rises would be structurally impossible. It is the tensile strength of steel that allows architects to defy gravity.

- **Bridges:** From Howrah Bridge in Kolkata to the modern cable-stayed bridges of China, steel enables connectivity over rivers, valleys, and oceans.
- **Smart Cities:** India's Smart City Mission relies heavily on steel for metro stations, underground tunnels, overhead flyovers, and modular housing.

What excites me is not just the present, but the **speed of transformation.** Traditional concrete buildings might take years; steel-intensive construction—such as **pre-engineered buildings (PEBs)**—can cut timelines in half, making India's urbanization faster, cheaper, and more efficient.

Steel in Mobility: Moving India Forward

Steel does not just stay rooted in our buildings; it moves with us every day.

- **Railways:** Indian Railways, one of the largest rail networks in the world, is built on steel. Tracks, coaches, and locomotives all rely on it. As India modernizes its railway infrastructure with high-speed trains and dedicated freight corridors, the demand for specialty steels will surge.
- **Automobiles:** From the Maruti Suzuki on your street to the electric cars of tomorrow, steel is the backbone of the auto industry. High-strength, lightweight steels are critical in making vehicles safer while reducing emissions.
- **Aviation & Shipping:** Aircraft use advanced steel alloys for landing gears and engines. Ships, which carry 90% of global trade, are floating giants of steel. India's shipping expansion, driven by Sagarmala and port-led growth, will only deepen this demand.

In short, every journey we take by road, rail, air, or sea rests on the resilience of steel.

Steel in Defense and Security

Nations are not built only with infrastructure; they are protected with strength. And in defense, steel plays a role that is strategic, silent, and non-negotiable.

- **Warships and Submarines:** India's naval expansion depends on specialized steel that can withstand pressure, saltwater, and combat conditions.
- **Tanks and Armored Vehicles:** The defense sector requires armor-grade steels that combine toughness with mobility.
- **Aerospace & Missiles:** Even in aerospace and defense technology, steel alloys find critical applications.

In fact, India has made remarkable strides in producing **defense-grade steels domestically,** reducing dependence on imports. This is not just industrial progress; it is national sovereignty forged in steel.

Steel in Industry & Energy

Every industry you can think of, whether it makes fertilizers, power, textiles, cement, or chemicals, relies on steel machinery, pipelines, and tools. Without steel, no other industry can thrive.

- **Power Sector:** Thermal plants, hydroelectric dams, wind turbines, solar panel mounts, all are steel-dependent.
- **Oil & Gas:** Pipelines carrying energy across thousands of kilometers are primarily made of steel.

- **Data Centers:** As India becomes a digital economy, even server racks, cooling systems, and modular centers are built using steel structures.

Steel is not just a passive participant here; it is the enabler of productivity itself.

Steel in Daily Life and Healthcare

If you think steel is only about industries and infrastructure, look again. It is also present in our homes and hospitals in subtle but vital ways.

- **Appliances:** Refrigerators, washing machines, and microwaves all have steel as their skeleton.
- **Healthcare:** Surgical instruments, hospital beds, MRI machines, and stents all depend on medical-grade stainless steel.
- **Lifestyles:** From the stainless steel utensils in every Indian household to the gyms we exercise in, steel quietly supports our well-being.

This daily relevance is why steel cannot be dismissed as "old economy." It may be ancient in discovery, but it remains futuristic in application.

The New Frontiers: Innovation in Steel Applications

What excites me most is how steel is reinventing itself.

- **High-Strength, Lightweight Steel:** Auto and aerospace industries are adopting steels that combine safety with efficiency.

- **Modular Housing:** Entire homes and offices are now being shipped as pre-engineered steel units.
- **Green Energy:** Steel is central to wind turbines and solar farms, meaning it is a key enabler of India's renewable future.
- **Medical Breakthroughs:** New alloys are being designed to work inside the human body without corrosion.

Steel is not stuck in the past; it is innovating alongside technology, finding new relevance in industries of tomorrow.

The Indispensable Backbone

When I look across these industries: infrastructure, mobility, defense, energy, healthcare, I see one truth. Every leap India wants to take in its development journey runs on the rails of steel.

If India wants to be a $5 trillion economy, steel is not optional; it is essential. It is the bridge between aspiration and achievement, between vision and reality.

That is why when we say "from pin to plane," it is not just a catchy phrase. It is the simplest way to capture a universal fact: **steel is the invisible backbone of everything around us.**

And as India rises, this backbone will only grow stronger.

CHAPTER 2

The Making of Steel

Steel is so deeply woven into our lives that we rarely stop to ask:

How is it actually made?

For most people, steel is simply "there" in buildings, cars, appliances, and infrastructure. But the process of making steel is as fascinating as the product itself. And understanding it, at least in simple terms, helps us see why steel holds such a unique position in the global economy, and why India has such a powerful role to play in its future.

From Earth to Industry: The Birth of Steel

At its core, **steel begins its life as iron ore,** one of the most abundant minerals on Earth. But raw iron is brittle and prone to corrosion. To transform it into something useful, humans discovered a method thousands of years ago: combining iron with small amounts of carbon (and later, other alloys like chromium, nickel, or manganese).

This is the magic: a little carbon turns fragile iron into strong, versatile, resilient steel.

The journey from ore to steel can be simplified into three main stages:

1. **Extracting Iron Ore:**
    - Mined from the earth, often in the form of hematite or magnetite.
    - India is blessed with rich reserves, particularly in Odisha, Jharkhand, and Chhattisgarh.
2. **Refining into Pig Iron:**
    - Iron ore is smelted in a blast furnace with coke (a form of carbon) and limestone.
    - This produces molten iron, also called pig iron, which is strong but brittle.
3. **Transforming into Steel:**
    - Pig iron is further refined in steel plants by reducing impurities (like sulfur, phosphorus) and controlling carbon content.
    - Additional alloys may be added depending on the type of steel required (stainless, structural, automotive-grade, etc.).

The end result is steel: a material that can be rolled into sheets, drawn into wires, or forged into beams and components.

Different Paths, One Destination

There isn't just one way to make steel. Over time, multiple technologies have evolved:

- **Blast Furnace–Basic Oxygen Furnace (BF-BOF):** The traditional method, large, capital-intensive, but efficient for mass production.

- **Electric Arc Furnace (EAF):** Uses electricity to melt scrap steel and convert it into new steel. This method is greener, since it recycles scrap and reduces carbon emissions.
- **Induction Furnace (IF):** Widely used in India by small and medium-scale producers. Less capital-intensive, ideal for catering to regional markets.

This variety is important. It means steel production can happen at both ends of the spectrum: massive integrated plants producing millions of tonnes, and nimble, regional units serving local demand.

India's Natural Advantage

India holds a unique position in the global steel story:

- **Raw Materials:** India is the world's second-largest producer of iron ore. This ensures the availability of key inputs domestically.
- **Young Workforce:** Steel production requires skilled yet labor-intensive processes. India's demographic dividend gives it an edge.
- **Growing Market:** With per-capita consumption at just ~77 kg, compared to China's 600+ kg, India's domestic demand is bound to rise for decades.
- **Cost Competitiveness:** India has some of the lowest production costs globally, making it an attractive hub for steel exports.

In many ways, India is standing at the same inflection point that China faced in the late 20th century, ready to use steel as the backbone of industrialization.

Why Understanding the Process Matters

For entrepreneurs and policymakers, steel production is not just a technical curiosity; it has real-world implications.

- **Energy Intensity:** Steelmaking is one of the most energy-intensive industries. Innovations in green energy and efficient furnaces can dramatically reduce costs.
- **Working Capital Cycles:** From iron ore to finished steel, the production cycle is long and cash-hungry. Managing these cycles well is often the difference between profit and bankruptcy for MSMEs.
- **Technology Choices:** The method chosen, blast furnace vs electric arc vs induction, affects capex, opex, and scalability.
- **Recycling Opportunities:** With steel being 100% recyclable, India has the chance to build a strong circular economy around scrap.

In other words, steel is not just about smelting and rolling. It is about strategic choices that ripple across business models, industries, and even national economies.

The Paradox of Steel: Old Yet Future-Ready

What fascinates me most is the paradox of steel.

On one hand, it is an ancient material used by civilizations for thousands of years. On the other hand, it is one of the most future-ready materials we have.

- **It adapts to new demands:** from skyscrapers to EVs, from space exploration to surgical implants.

- **It aligns with sustainability goals:** 100% recyclable, infinitely reusable.
- **It supports industrialization:** no modern industry can thrive without it.

Unlike many "sunset" industries that fade with time, steel is a **sunrise sector hiding in plain sight.**

I chose to dedicate an entire chapter to the making of steel, not to teach metallurgy, but to highlight a simple truth:

Steel is not a commodity; it is a carefully engineered product that requires vision, discipline, and strategic thinking.

When I meet entrepreneurs in the steel space, I remind them:

"You're not just melting iron; you're shaping the backbone of India's future."

As we move ahead, understanding both the **science of steelmaking** and the economics behind it will be crucial in positioning India as a global leader in this industry.

Because in the story of nations, those who control steel control growth.

□ □ □

CHAPTER 3

India vs China: The Usage Gap

One of the simplest ways to understand the scale of opportunity in steel is to compare India with its neighbor, China. For decades, China has been the world's largest consumer and producer of steel, using it as the backbone of its transformation from an agrarian economy to a manufacturing and infrastructure powerhouse.

India, despite being the **second-largest producer** of steel, lags far behind in terms of **per-capita consumption.** And it is here that the story gets interesting.

The Numbers That Tell the Story

Let's look at the data.

Metric	India (2023)	China (2023)	Global Average
Per Capita Steel Consumption	~77 kg	~630 kg	~240 kg
Total Production	~125 million tonnes	~1,000 million tonnes+	~1950 million tonnes
Share of Global Steel Output	~6%	~54%	—

These numbers are not just statistics. They are signposts of economic maturity.

- China consumes over **eight times more steel per person** than India.
- Even the **global average** is more than three times India's level.
- And yet, India is the **second-largest producer.**

This gap between **production and consumption** is both a challenge and an opportunity.

The China Playbook: How Steel Built a Superpower

China's economic miracle over the past 40 years cannot be explained without steel.

- In the 1980s, China consumed less than 100 kg of steel per capita, similar to India today.
- As China embarked on its manufacturing boom, urbanization, and infrastructure spree, steel consumption surged past 500 kg per person by the 2000s.
- Every bridge, every apartment block, every factory, every shipyard—steel was the silent partner in this transformation.

By the mid-2010s, China was consuming more than half the world's steel output. This single factor reshaped global trade, shipping, and raw material supply chains.

India's Position: The Sleeping Giant

India today looks eerily similar to where China stood in the 1980s.

- **Rapid urbanization:** By 2030, 40% of Indians will live in cities.
- **Infrastructure push:** Highways, expressways, metro networks, airports, all steel-intensive.
- **Manufacturing drive:** Initiatives like Make in India and PLI schemes are boosting sectors that rely heavily on steel.
- **Housing demand:** India will need 70–80 million new homes by 2035, most of them steel-reinforced.

In other words, India's steel demand story is just beginning.

The Opportunity Gap

Let's imagine what happens if India's steel consumption rises even modestly.

- At 77 kg per capita × 1.4 billion people, India consumes ~108 million tonnes domestically.
- If India were to double consumption to 150 kg per capita, demand would jump to 210 million tonnes.
- If India were to reach just half of China's level (300 kg per capita), demand would cross 420 million tonnes, almost 4x today's levels.

This is not a distant dream; it is a trajectory already underway.

The multiplier effect of urbanization + industrialization + rising incomes will drive steel into every sector of the economy.

Steel and GDP: A Clear Correlation

Globally, there is a strong correlation between per-capita steel consumption and GDP per capita.

- **Low-income countries:** <100 kg per capita.
- **Middle-income countries:** 200–400 kg per capita.
- **High-income countries:** 500–800 kg per capita.

India's GDP per capita (~$2,600) and steel usage (~77 kg) place it firmly in the **early development stage.** As GDP grows, steel usage will inevitably follow.

This is why I call steel a leading indicator of growth. If you want to predict where a country's economy is headed, don't just look at GDP; look at steel consumption.

Why the Gap Exists

Several factors explain why India's consumption lags:

1. **Rural Economy Dominance:** A large share of India's population still lives in rural areas with low steel usage.
2. **Infrastructure Deficit:** Highways, bridges, and metros are still catching up with demand.
3. **Housing Patterns:** India has traditionally relied on brick-and-mortar rather than steel-intensive housing.
4. **Industrial Base:** Manufacturing's share in GDP remains ~17%, compared to 30%+ in China.

But these are not permanent constraints; they are areas of imminent growth.

The Multiplier Effect of Catching Up

Every tonne of additional steel consumption creates a ripple effect:

- Jobs in mining, logistics, and manufacturing.
- Demand for allied industries like cement, power, and construction.
- Exports of finished steel products to global markets.

Steel is not just about supply; it's about **economic acceleration.**

If India narrows the usage gap with China, it will not just be about more steel. It will mean more jobs, stronger infrastructure, faster mobility, and a sturdier industrial backbone.

The Gap as Gold

When I look at the numbers, I don't see India's steel story as "behind China." I see it as **ahead of time.**

Because while China has already reached maturity, India still has the runway ahead. Every kilogram of steel per person that India adds is another step toward prosperity.

This is why I call the usage gap India's goldmine of opportunity.

For entrepreneurs, investors, and policymakers, the message is clear: if you want to build wealth in the coming decades, look where the gap is largest and the potential is highest.

And in India today, that gap is in steel.

□ □ □

CHAPTER 4

Steel Across Industries

When we say "steel is everywhere," it's not just a catchy phrase; it's reality. From the roads we drive on, to the cars we use, to the buildings we live and work in, to the very defense systems that secure our borders, steel is embedded in every aspect of modern life.

But to truly grasp its importance, we must break it down industry by industry. Each sector tells a story of how steel is not only a raw material but a strategic enabler of growth.

1. Pre-Engineered Buildings (PEBs): The Silent Revolution

If there is one area of steel that excites me the most, it is PEBs.

What are PEBs? Factory-fabricated steel structures, assembled on-site.

- **Benefits:** 50% faster construction, cost savings, flexibility, and durability.
- **Applications:** Warehouses, industrial sheds, cold storage, malls, airports, stadiums, and even schools.
- **Why this matters:** India's growth story in the next decade will not be slow and incremental—it will be fast and ambitious. Nothing demonstrates this better than the recent news: India has officially applied to host the 2030

Commonwealth Games and submitted a bid to host the 2036 Summer Olympics in Ahmedabad.

If India is to prepare for such global events, it will require the rapid development of world-class infrastructure: stadiums, housing, logistics parks, airports, and supporting facilities. Traditional construction methods cannot meet these timelines. PEBs will.

- **Market Projection:** The Indian PEB market is expected to reach $25 billion by 2030, growing at over 10% annually. With e-commerce, logistics, and industrial parks booming, every warehouse for Amazon, Flipkart, or Reliance Retail is essentially a PEB.
- **Opportunity for entrepreneurs:** From supplying fabricated steel to offering design, assembly, and logistics services, the PEB revolution will open doors for thousands of MSMEs.

PEBs symbolize the speed of growth India aspires to achieve—quick, efficient, and scalable. And steel is the engine that makes this possible.

2. Infrastructure: The Foundation of Progress

Infrastructure is perhaps the single biggest consumer of steel worldwide—and in India, it will define the next two decades.

- **Current Usage:** Roughly 60–65% of India's total steel demand comes from infrastructure and construction.
- **Examples:** Bridges, highways, metro rail projects, airports, and ports.

- **Government Push:** The National Infrastructure Pipeline (NIP) targets over $1.4 trillion of investments by 2030.
- **Flagship Projects:** Bharatmala highways, Sagarmala port upgrades, bullet train corridors, and Smart Cities Mission—all steel-heavy.
- **Why this matters:** Every kilometer of highway requires ~1,600 tonnes of steel. Every kilometer of metro rail uses ~5,000 tonnes. India plans to expand its highways by 25,000 km and metro lines by 7,000 km in the coming decade. That's millions of tonnes of demand locked in.
- **Opportunity for entrepreneurs:** MSMEs can participate by supplying fabricated steel, construction-grade products, or even logistics services for moving steel to project sites.

3. Housing & Urban Development: The Shelter Revolution

India's housing market is undergoing a seismic shift.

- **Steel Usage in Housing:** From TMT bars for reinforcement to steel roofing, window frames, and modular construction.
- **Demand Drivers:** Urban migration, affordable housing schemes, and the rise of high-rise apartments.
- **Government Push:** The Pradhan Mantri Awas Yojana aims to build over 20 million affordable homes.
- **Why this matters:** Traditional brick-and-mortar housing is slow and resource-intensive. Steel-intensive construction, especially pre-engineered buildings (PEBs) and modular housing, allows faster, cheaper, and more durable homes.
- **Future Edge:** In the next 15 years, India will need 70–80 million new homes. If even 25% adopt steel-intensive

construction, the demand for structural steel will grow exponentially.

4. Automobiles & Electric Vehicles (EVs): The Mobility Frontier

The auto industry is one of the most dynamic steel consumers.

- **Current Contribution:** ~10–12% of total steel demand in India.
- **Applications:** Body frames, chassis, panels, gears, bearings, wheels, and safety reinforcements.
- **EV Opportunity:** Electric vehicles require lightweight, high-strength steel to improve efficiency and range.
- **Why this matters:** India's auto sector is expected to grow from $118 billion today to $300 billion by 2030. With EV penetration rising, demand for specialty steels like high-tensile and silicon steels will surge.
- **Global Parallel:** China's EV boom (BYD, Nio, SAIC) was supported by a massive domestic steel supply chain. India will follow a similar trajectory, and entrepreneurs in the auto supply chain can benefit immensely.

5. Defense & Aerospace: Securing the Nation

Steel is not just about growth; it's also about security.

- **Applications:** Tanks, warships, submarines, fighter aircraft, missiles, and border infrastructure.
- **Special Steels:** Ballistic steel, maraging steel, and stainless steel grades designed for defense applications.

- **Indigenization Push:** The government's Atmanirbhar Bharat policy encourages domestic defense production.
- **Why this matters:** India has the world's third-largest defense budget. As procurement shifts from imports to domestic manufacturing, the demand for high-grade defense steels will rise dramatically.
- **Opportunity for MSMEs:** Defense PSUs and private players like L&T, Tata Advanced Systems, and HAL require specialized steel components, creating opportunities for niche suppliers.

6. Renewable Energy & Sustainability: Building a Green Future

Steel is at the heart of India's green transition.

- **Wind Energy:** Steel makes up ~80% of a wind turbine by weight.
- **Solar Farms:** Mounting structures and trackers are steel-intensive.
- **Hydrogen Economy:** Specialized steels will be critical for hydrogen storage and pipelines.
- **Why this matters:** India targets 500 GW of renewable energy by 2030. Every gigawatt of wind or solar energy requires thousands of tonnes of steel.

In fact, the energy transition is also a steel transition.

7. Data Centers & Digital Infrastructure: The New-Age Driver

The digital economy may feel weightless, but it runs on steel.

Applications:

- **Data Centers:** Racks, frames, cooling systems, and even building structures are steel-intensive.
- **5G Towers:** Require high-strength galvanized steel.
- **AI & Cloud:** The physical infrastructure that powers "Digital India" is made of steel.
- **Market Projection:** India's data center capacity is expected to grow 6x by 2030. This is a hidden but massive driver of demand.

The Steel Multiplier

When we examine steel across industries, a clear pattern emerges:

- It is not just a raw material.
- It is an enabler of transformation across every sector.

From PEBs and infrastructure to housing, autos, defense, renewables, and digital infrastructure, each is a growth engine powered by steel.

The coming decade, especially with India's global ambitions like hosting the Commonwealth Games and Olympics, will demand s**peed, scale, and strength.** PEBs will be the face of this rapid development, but every sector will ride the same wave.

For entrepreneurs, the lesson is simple: Instead of chasing industries that are flashy but fragile, build your business in industries that are foundational and future-proof. And steel is at the heart of them all.

This is why I say: **Steel is not just the new gold, it is the currency of growth.**

CHAPTER 5

Sustainability: Steel vs Plastic

When we talk about the industries of the future, one word keeps coming up: sustainability. The world is becoming increasingly conscious of climate change, waste management, and environmental degradation. Nations, businesses, and consumers are now rethinking how products are made, used, and disposed of.

And in this conversation, **two materials stand on opposite sides of the spectrum: plastic and steel.**

Plastic: The Convenience That Became a Crisis

Plastic was once celebrated as the wonder material of the 20th century. Lightweight, versatile, and cheap, it revolutionized packaging, transportation, and consumer goods. But over time, the same qualities that made it attractive created a crisis.

- **Non-Biodegradable:** Most plastics take 500–1,000 years to decompose.
- **Low Recycling Rate:** Less than 10% of the world's plastic is recycled effectively.
- **Pollution:** India alone generates over 3.5 million tonnes of plastic waste annually, and a large portion ends up in landfills, rivers, and oceans.

- **Health Risks:** Microplastics are now found in food, water, and even human bloodstreams.

Plastic was a shortcut solution for industrial and consumer needs—but its afterlife is a nightmare.

Steel: The Original Sustainable Material

Steel, in contrast, is not only strong and versatile but also one of the most environmentally friendly materials ever created.

- **100% Recyclable:** Steel can be recycled indefinitely without losing its properties.
- **Recycling Rate:** Globally, around 85–90% of all steel is recycled, making it the world's most recycled material.
- **Energy Savings:** Recycling steel saves about 74% of the energy compared to making new steel from raw ore.
- **Circular Economy Champion:** Every tonne of steel recycled saves 1.5 tonnes of CO_2 emissions, 1.4 tonnes of iron ore, and 740 kg of coal.

In fact, the spoon you eat with today may have been part of a ship or a bridge decades ago. That's the magic of steel; it never truly dies.

India's Plastic Problem vs Steel's Opportunity

India faces a massive environmental challenge: rising plastic consumption and poor waste management infrastructure.

- Urban India is drowning in single-use plastic packaging.
- Small businesses and consumers still depend heavily on low-cost plastic.

- Waste segregation and recycling remain inefficient.

This is where steel steps in as a solution.

- **Packaging Alternatives:** Steel cans and containers are safer, stronger, and recyclable.
- **Consumer Goods:** Stainless steel utensils, bottles, and straws are re-emerging as eco-friendly replacements for plastic.
- **Infrastructure:** Steel pipes and fittings last decades longer than plastic alternatives, reducing replacement waste.

By shifting even a fraction of demand from plastic to steel, India can dramatically reduce waste and align with global sustainability standards.

The Return of Steel in Daily Life

The Current Sustainability Scenario

A few years ago, plastic bottles and straws dominated households. But growing awareness and bans on single-use plastics have triggered a comeback of stainless steel bottles, lunch boxes, and cutlery.

- Startups are now branding steel products as "eco-luxury."
- Schools and offices increasingly encourage reusable steel containers.
- Even restaurants are adopting steel straws and tumblers.

This trend signals not nostalgia, but a new market shift, where sustainability is not a compromise, but a business opportunity.

Global Sustainability Standards: India Cannot Ignore

Globally, steel is being positioned as a key pillar of the green economy:

- **Europe:** The European Union is pushing for "green steel" using hydrogen instead of coal.
- **Middle East:** Dubai's skyline is not only steel-heavy but also designed with recyclability in mind.
- **Japan & South Korea:** Leaders in high-efficiency recycling systems, where steel plays a central role.

As India seeks to be part of global supply chains, adopting sustainable steel practices will no longer be optional; it will be essential.

Steel vs Plastic: A Comparison Table

Factor	Plastic	Steel
Lifespan	1–10 years (depending on product)	50–100+ years (in infrastructure)
Recyclability	<10% effectively recycled	85–90% globally recycled
Environmental Impact	Pollutes land, water, and air	Minimal, as recycling is effective
Economic Value	Low scrap value	High scrap value
Health Impact	Microplastic contamination	Non-toxic, safe for food contact

The contrast is stark.

Where plastic creates problems, steel creates solutions.

Entrepreneurial Opportunities in Sustainability

The push towards eco-friendly solutions is not just a moral imperative; it's a **market opportunity.**

- **Steel Packaging Startups:** Offering alternatives to plastic bottles and cans.
- **Recycling Businesses:** Collecting and reprocessing scrap steel profitably.
- **Eco-Brands:** Positioning stainless steel products as modern lifstyle choices.
- **Green Infrastructure:** Building long-lasting steel-intensive projects reduces environmental costs.

As consumers, corporates, and governments align on sustainability, steel-based businesses will naturally benefit.

Steel as the Sustainable Future

The debate between steel and plastic is not really a debate—it is a reality check.

Plastic was a convenient shortcut that has overstayed its welcome. Steel, by contrast, has stood the test of time, not just for strength, but for **sustainability.**

In a world racing towards net-zero goals and circular economies, steel offers something rare: a material that is strong, affordable, and infinitely recyclable.

For entrepreneurs, the message is clear: **Build businesses around steel, and you are building for both profit and planet.**

And that is why, in the sustainability story of the 21st century, **steel is the hero India needs.**

□ □ □

CHAPTER 6

Global Edge & Indian Potential

Whenever I travel abroad, I pay special attention to one thing: the skyline. Because skylines tell stories. They reveal the ambition of a nation, the scale of its economy, and the materials that hold it all together.

And in almost every global megacity, Dubai, New York, Singapore, Shanghai, one material dominates those skylines: **steel.**

Steel is not just the backbone of infrastructure; it is a symbol of modernity, ambition, and economic power.

Dubai: The City Built on Steel Dreams

Few places in the world demonstrate the power of steel like Dubai.

- The Burj Khalifa, the tallest building in the world, stands 828 meters high. Its frame required 31,400 metric tonnes of steel rebar.
- Dubai Metro, spanning over 70 km, is almost entirely steel-reinforced.
- Palm Jumeirah & Dubai Marina, iconic man-made marvels, depend on advanced steel engineering to withstand environmental stress.

What's remarkable is the pace: Dubai transformed from a desert trading outpost to a global metropolis in less than 30 years. And the enabler was steel—allowing fast, flexible, and futuristic construction.

Lesson for India

If India aspires to build world-class cities under Smart Cities and urban renewal missions, steel must be the primary driver.

China: The Benchmark in Consumption

When it comes to steel, no country compares to China.

- **Per Capita Consumption:** ~630 kg per person annually (vs ~77 kg in India).
- **Output:** China produces over 1 billion tonnes of steel annually—more than half of global output.
- **Urbanization:** 600+ cities transformed into modern hubs, powered by steel-intensive housing, metro systems, bridges, and industrial zones.
- **Export Edge:** China doesn't just use steel; it exports value-added products like machinery, cars, and electronics built on steel.

Lesson for India

Our consumption gap is not a weakness, but an untapped opportunity. If India doubles per capita consumption to just 150 kg, it will require an additional 100 **million tonnes of steel annually.** That alone would rewrite global demand equations.

Japan & South Korea: Masters of Innovation

While they cannot match China in size, Japan and South Korea dominate in quality and innovation.

- **High-Grade Steels:** Used in shipbuilding, electronics, automotive, and defense.
- **Efficiency:** Japan's steel plants are among the world's most energy-efficient.
- **Technology Exports:** South Korea's POSCO is a global steel leader, setting benchmarks in process optimization and green steel initiatives.

Lesson for India

We must not only expand production but also climb the value chain, moving from basic steel to advanced alloys, specialty steels, and green steel.

Europe: Leading the Green Steel Revolution

Europe may not lead in volume, but it leads in vision.

- **Green Steel Initiatives:** Companies like SSAB (Sweden) and ArcelorMittal are producing hydrogen-based steel, reducing dependence on coal.
- **Circular Economy:** Nearly all structural steel in Europe is recycled or repurposed.
- **Policy Push:** The EU's Carbon Border Adjustment Mechanism (CBAM) will penalize high-emission steel imports, encouraging cleaner production globally.

Lesson for India

If we want to integrate into global supply chains, especially exports, Indian steel must meet global sustainability standards.

India's Current Position

India today is the second-largest producer of steel in the world, but there's a paradox:

- **Production:** ~125 million tonnes annually.
- **Consumption:** Only ~77 kg per capita, among the lowest for a major economy.
- **Exports:** Mostly raw or semi-finished steel, not high-value finished goods.
- **Industry Fragmentation:** Many small players operate with outdated technology and low efficiency.

Yet, these gaps are hidden opportunities.

The Potential for India: Why the Time is Now

1. **Urbanization:** By 2035, 600 million Indians will live in cities. Steel-intensive housing, metros, and infrastructure are inevitable.
2. **Manufacturing Push:** "Make in India" + PLI schemes will boost auto, defense, and electronics, all steel-heavy industries.
3. **Renewables:** Solar, wind, and hydrogen projects require massive steel inputs.

4. **Exports:** With global buyers looking for China+1 alternatives, India can emerge as a reliable steel supplier.
5. **Sustainability Advantage:** If India adopts green steel early, it can bypass older, inefficient models and leapfrog into leadership.

A Comparative Snapshot

Country	Per Capita Steel Use (kg)	Annual Production (MT)	Key Strength
China	~630	~1000+	Scale & infrastructure
Japan	~500	~100	High-grade steels & efficiency
South Korea	~1000+	~70	Technology & innovation
Europe (avg.)	~350	~150	Green steel & recycling
India	~77	~125	Scale potential, low consumption

This table shows one thing very clearly: India is not behind; it is under-utilized.

The headroom for growth is massive.

The Global Edge Meets Indian Potential

The global examples, from Dubai's steel skyline to Europe's green steel, from China's massive consumption to Japan's innovation, are not just stories. They are roadmaps.

India's opportunity lies in combining these lessons:

- Scale like China.
- Innovate like Japan.
- Sustain like Europe.
- Build ambitiously like Dubai.

If India follows this integrated approach, we won't just be the second-largest producer of steel. We can be the largest, most sustainable, and most valuable steel economy in the world.

The Indian Steel Moment

Every global success story in steel shows us one truth: steel builds nations.

- Dubai used it to announce itself to the world.
- China used it to transform villages into megacities.
- Japan and Korea used it to export value-added products.
- Europe used it to lead in sustainability.

Now it's India's turn.

With rising demand, government support, and entrepreneurial energy, India stands at the edge of a steel revolution. This is not just about catching up; it is about leapfrogging.

And if we seize this moment, steel will not only be the backbone of India's growth, it will be our ticket to global leadership.

□ □ □

CHAPTER 7

Why Steel Will Be the Next Gold

Gold has always held a special place in human history. It is shiny, rare, and universally accepted as a symbol of wealth. From ancient kings to modern investors, gold has been treasured as a store of value.

However, here's the truth: **gold may preserve wealth, but it does not create it.**

- If you bury gold in the ground today and return after 50 years, it will remain gold, **unchanged, but also unproductive.**
- Steel, on the other hand, is the opposite. **Steel, when put to work, builds wealth.** It creates factories, bridges, cars, ships, homes, and entire cities.

That is why I believe: **Steel is the new gold.**

Gold: A Store of Value, But Not a Driver of Growth

Let's start with gold.

- **Global Value:** The world holds around 200,000 tonnes of mined gold. Its primary role is jewelry, central bank reserves, and as an inflation hedge.
- **India's Obsession:** India alone holds over 25,000 tonnes of gold, mostly in households. That's more than the official reserves of the U.S., Germany, and Italy combined.

- **Economic Role:** Yet, gold's role in the economy is passive. It does not produce, it does not employ, it does not build.

Gold is, in many ways, static wealth. It shines, but it doesn't scale.

Steel: The Creator of Value

Now contrast that with steel.

- **Every $1 spent on steel in infrastructure creates $6–8 in GDP value** through multiplier effects.
- Steel is directly linked to **urbanization, industrialization, and national defense.**
- It is both the **foundation** (bridges, factories, housing) and the enabler (cars, metros, ships, defense systems).
- Every tonne of steel consumed creates jobs—not just in plants, but across supply chains: logistics, construction, automotive, and beyond.

Unlike gold, steel is not stored; it is circulated, multiplied, and transformed into wealth.

Steel as Strategic Wealth

Nations that have mastered steel have mastered growth.

- **The U.S. in the 20th century:** Steel built railroads, skyscrapers, and warships, enabling America's rise as a superpower.
- **China in the 21st century:** Its steel consumption turned a developing economy into the world's second-largest GDP.

- **India's moment:** We are at the threshold of a similar leap, where steel demand will accelerate our journey to becoming a $10 trillion economy.

Steel, unlike gold, is strategic wealth.

It defines power, capability, and competitiveness on the world stage.

The Per Capita Test: Gold vs Steel

Consider two statistics:

- **Gold:** India has one of the highest gold holdings per capita globally, yet we are still a developing economy.
- **Steel:** India's steel consumption per capita is just ~77 kg, compared to 630+ kg in China.

If wealth were truly about gold, India should already be one of the richest nations on earth. But real prosperity correlates with steel consumption, not gold accumulation.

The lesson is clear: **gold is cultural wealth, steel is economic wealth.**

Steel and the Indian Dream

India's aspirations for a $5 trillion GDP, world-class cities, self-reliant defense, EV leadership, etc., cannot be built with gold. They require steel.

- **Smart Cities:** steel-intensive infrastructure.
- **Affordable Housing:** steel-driven modular construction.
- **EV Factories:** specialty steels for lightweight and efficient vehicles.

- **Defense Manufacturing:** high-grade steels for tanks, ships, and aerospace.
- **Renewables:** turbines, solar frames, and hydrogen pipelines—all steel-heavy.

Steel, in short, is the currency of development.

Why Steel is the New Gold for Entrepreneurs

For business owners and MSMEs, steel represents a far more powerful opportunity than gold.

- **Gold locks capital.** Steel unlocks industries.
- **Gold sits idle.** Steel creates cash flows.
- **Gold is scarce.** Steel is scalable.

When entrepreneurs invest in steel-intensive industries, be it pre-engineered buildings, automotive parts, logistics, or defense, they are building not just businesses, but **nation-building enterprises.**

This is why, as an investor and advisor, I guide entrepreneurs to focus **on industries of necessity,** and steel tops that list.

A Visionary Comparison: Gold Mines vs Steel Plants

- A gold mine produces wealth for a few shareholders.
- A steel plant produces wealth for thousands: workers, suppliers, transporters, builders, and the larger economy.
- Gold mines deplete with extraction. Steel plants scale with innovation.

The value creation is incomparable.

A nation full of steel plants will always outperform a nation full of gold mines.

Steel is the Wealth Multiplier of the Future

We respect gold for its cultural and financial role. It will always have its place in jewelry and central bank vaults. But if we are talking about building futures, creating jobs, and driving growth, the crown belongs to steel.

- Gold is wealth preserved.
- Steel is wealth produced.
- Gold shines.
- Steel builds.

And that is why, in the India of tomorrow, steel is the new gold.

□ □ □

CHAPTER 8

Your Playbook for Scaling in the Steel Industry

Over the years, I have worked with hundreds of entrepreneurs, many from the steel value chain. Some succeeded spectacularly, while others struggled despite the same market opportunities. What separated them was not luck, but the way they managed **capital, operations, and scalability.**

Steel is a capital-intensive industry, but that does not mean only giants like Tata Steel or JSW can dominate.

In fact, I believe the real wealth creation will happen through agile, smart, and efficient MSMEs who learn to play the steel game right.

Here is a playbook that I have created specifically for this purpose:

A set of principles and strategies that can help entrepreneurs scale sustainably in this industry.

1. Master Working Capital Management

The steel industry is notorious for cash flow crunches. Prices fluctuate, payment cycles are long, and inventory needs are heavy.

- **Don't just chase sales; chase cash:** Many entrepreneurs boast about top-line growth, but what matters is cash in the bank.
- **Negotiate supplier credit:** Building strong relationships with suppliers can give you 30–60 days of breathing space.
- **Invoice discounting:** Platforms like Capital Setu (which we built) help MSMEs unlock cash tied in receivables. If your customers pay in 90 days, you can still get liquidity today.
- **Keep a rolling forecast:** Always know your inflows and outflows for the next 90 days. Steel markets can be volatile; you must plan ahead.

Working capital is the oxygen of your business. Without it, even profitable businesses suffocate.

2. Go Asset-Light Where Possible

Traditional thinking says you need to own massive plants and machinery to succeed in steel.

That's not always true.

- **Contract manufacturing:** Instead of investing in heavy capex, many MSMEs can outsource production during the initial stages.
- **Shared infrastructure:** Industrial parks and clusters often provide common utilities, cutting costs.
- **Focus on distribution and design:** Sometimes, value-added services like fabrication, logistics, or engineered design create more margin than owning a blast furnace.

Remember, every rupee locked in machinery is a rupee not available for scaling.

Smart entrepreneurs stay flexible.

3. Optimize Utilization: The Power of 3 Shifts

One of the simplest yet most overlooked secrets in manufacturing is utilization.

- A plant that runs one shift is only using ~33% of its capacity.
- Two shifts take you to ~66%.
- Three shifts unlock 90%+ efficiency, spreading fixed costs thin and boosting profitability.

This requires proper manpower planning, maintenance schedules, and incentives.

However, the principle is clear: **better utilization beats expansion.**

Many steel businesses fail because they chase new capacity without maximizing what they already have.

4. Produce More with Less Capex

Steel is often seen as a "big boys' game" because of high entry barriers. But technology and modular designs are changing that.

- Mini mills and induction furnaces allow smaller setups at lower investment.
- Pre-engineered building (PEB) units are far less capital-heavy than conventional construction.
- Automation and digital tools help even mid-sized players scale without proportionate manpower increases.

The mindset shift is: don't grow by spending more—grow by using what you have better.

5. Build Moats with Value-Added Products

Raw steel trading has wafer-thin margins.

The real money lies in value addition.

- **Fabrication services** (cutting, welding, assembly) add both margin and stickiness.
- **Specialized steels** (for defense, EVs, aerospace) offer higher profits than commodity steel.
- Integration with MSMEs. For example, supplying custom steel parts for auto or rail creates long-term contracts.

Your goal should not be to compete on price, but to compete on problem-solving.

6. Leverage Technology & Data

Most MSMEs in steel run their businesses traditionally.

However, the future will belong to those who embrace data.

- **Track input-output ratios.** Small inefficiencies compound into massive costs over time.
- **Adopt ERP systems.** Even simple cloud tools can reduce leakages.
- **Predict demand.** Market analytics can help you stock the right products at the right time, avoiding dead inventory.
- **Use AI in logistics.** Optimizing truck routes and fuel costs can make or break profitability in steel supply chains.

Steel may be an old industry, but tech-first MSMEs will be the disruptors.

7. Diversify, But with Focus

Steel demand is spread across multiple sectors: construction, auto, defense, renewables, and infrastructure.

- Don't depend entirely on one sector. If the auto industry slows down, construction might still be booming.
- But don't stretch too thin either. Choose 2–3 sectors where your expertise is strongest.
- Build sector-specific knowledge. For example, supplying to defense requires understanding certifications, while auto requires just-in-time delivery systems.

Focused diversification builds resilience without diluting capability.

8. Think Beyond India: Steel as a Global Play

The Indian steel story is powerful, but global opportunities are even bigger.

- **Middle East:** Massive infrastructure expansion; Dubai, Saudi Arabia's Vision 2030.
- **Africa:** Demand for affordable housing and roads is rising sharply.
- **Southeast Asia:** Smaller nations look to import because domestic production is limited.

Even MSMEs can tap into these markets through exports, joint ventures, or supply chains.

Steel is not just local; it's global.

9. Culture & Leadership in Steel Businesses

At the end of the day, scaling is not just about numbers; it's about people.

- **Retain skilled workers.** In steel, experience matters. A welder or furnace operator with 10 years of expertise can save you crores by preventing downtime.
- **Train continuously.** As technology changes, your team must evolve.
- **Create ownership.** Incentivize managers with performance-linked rewards so they treat the plant like their own.

Steel businesses with strong cultures withstand market shocks better than those built only on opportunism.

Scaling Smart, Not Just Big

The steel industry is vast, but also unforgiving. Many have lost fortunes chasing scale without strategy. But those who respect capital, optimize utilization, leverage technology, and build resilient teams will thrive.

In my years of working with entrepreneurs, I've learned this: you don't need to be the biggest to be the most profitable. You need to be the smartest.

And in steel, the smartest businesses will be the ones that follow this playbook, balancing strength with flexibility, ambition with discipline, and vision with execution.

Steel is the new gold, but only for those who learn how to mine its potential wisely.

□ □ □

CHAPTER 9

The Future We Must Build

When I look at India today, I see a nation standing at a historic crossroads. On one side, we have the legacy of being a primarily agrarian and service-driven economy. On the other hand, we have the unprecedented opportunity to become the **world's factory, builder, and innovator.** And at the very foundation of this transformation lies one simple material: steel.

This chapter is not just about data and projections; it is about vision. A vision for India, for our entrepreneurs, for our MSMEs, and for the global role we must claim.

Steel: The Backbone of India's Growth Story

Think about the transformation India has already witnessed in the last 25 years:

- From a country where owning a car was a luxury, to one of the fastest-growing auto markets in the world.
- From limited metro networks to sprawling urban transport systems in over 25 cities.
- From modest infrastructure to world-class airports, expressways, and data centers.

Each of these milestones has been made possible by steel.

Now, imagine the next 25 years:

- High-speed rail networks connecting all major cities.
- Green energy hubs with massive wind and solar farms.
- Defense self-reliance, where India produces its own ships, tanks, and aircraft.
- Affordable housing for all, built faster and stronger with pre-engineered steel structures.

The common thread? **Steel is the non-negotiable foundation.**

Why I Believe Steel Is the New Gold

Gold has always been considered valuable because it is rare, shiny, and a store of wealth. But I argue that steel is far more valuable for building a nation's future.

- Gold sits in vaults. Steel builds economies.
- Gold signals wealth. Steel creates wealth.
- Gold is tradition. Steel is progress.

When I say steel is the new gold, I mean that it is not just an industrial commodity; it is the currency of growth. Nations that control steel control their destiny.

India's Window of Opportunity

For decades, China has been the uncontested giant in steel. But the world is now looking for **the next growth engine.** Supply chains are shifting, geopolitical dynamics are changing, and India is emerging as the natural alternative.

Here are the facts:

- India consumes only ~77 kg of steel per person, compared to China's ~630 kg.
- Even if India doubles its per capita consumption to just ~150 kg in the next decade, it will require **hundreds of millions of tons of additional steel.**
- The government's push through *Atmanirbhar Bharat* and *Make in India* is creating massive demand in infrastructure, defense, and energy.

This is not just an opportunity; it is a national mission.

The Entrepreneur's Role in the Steel Revolution

Large corporations will, of course, play their part. But the real momentum will come from MSMEs.

- Small and mid-sized steel fabricators who serve the auto industry.
- Contractors who build warehouses, factories, and logistics parks.
- Suppliers who design specialized steel components for renewable energy projects.
- Exporters who tap into markets in Africa, the Middle East, and Southeast Asia.

The steel revolution will not be driven by a few; it will be powered by **thousands of entrepreneurs** who seize this moment.

This is why I believe MSMEs must stop chasing short-term trends and start aligning with industries of necessity, and steel is at the very top of that list.

Sustainability & The Green Steel Imperative

The future is not just about producing more; it is about producing responsibly.

- **Steel is 100% recyclable.** Unlike plastic, it can be reused indefinitely without losing quality.
- **Green steel technologies such as** hydrogen-based production, carbon capture, and energy-efficient furnaces are not luxuries; they will soon be mandatory.
- India has the chance to leapfrog older methods and become a leader in sustainable steel.

The **global economy is moving toward carbon-neutral commitments.** If Indian businesses invest in green steel now, they won't just meet domestic demand; they will become exporters to the world.

My Advice to Entrepreneurs Entering the Steel Space

Having worked with countless businesses, I want to leave you with some timeless principles:

1. **Think long-term.** Steel is not about quick wins; it is about building resilient, generational businesses.
2. **Stay asset-light initially.** Don't sink all your capital into plants; focus on partnerships and value addition.
3. **Invest in people.** Skilled welders, designers, and operators are your true assets.

4. **Adopt technology early.** Data, AI, automation—these are not optional in the next decade.
5. **Diversify smartly.** Don't put all your bets on one sector; balance between infra, auto, defense, and exports.

Steel rewards discipline, patience, and vision, the same qualities that define great entrepreneurs.

A Call to Action: Building the Future Together

The next decade will define whether India remains a service-driven economy or transforms into a global industrial leader. Steel will decide that outcome.

As entrepreneurs, policymakers, and investors, we have a choice:

- We can continue treating steel as just another commodity.
- Or we can embrace it as the **new gold; the foundation of wealth, strength, and progress.**

I have bet my vision on the latter. And I invite you to do the same.

- The world is looking for the next growth story.
- Let us make sure that story is "India".
- Because when the world builds its future, it will be built on steel.

Stay Connected

This book is only the beginning of the conversation. The real impact will come from collaboration:

- Entrepreneurs sharing their ideas
- Policymakers shaping frameworks
- And investors placing bold bets on industries of necessity like steel.

If you are an entrepreneur looking to scale, an investor seeking opportunities, or a policymaker committed to India's growth story, I would be glad to connect and continue the dialogue.

You can reach me at:

Write to me: pankaj.goel@capitalsetu.com

Connect on WhatsApp (EA to the Author): +91 96509 38009

Together, let us build India's future: stronger, faster, and better.

Because steel is not just the new gold: It is the foundation on which India's tomorrow will rise.